W9-BFE-804

BOYCOTTING THE BRITISH

BOSTON TEA PARTY

Virginia Loh-Hagan

45th Parallel Press

Published in the United States of America by Cherry Lake Publishing
Ann Arbor, Michigan
www.cherrylakepublishing.com

Reading Adviser: Marla Conn MS, Ed., Literacy specialist, Read-Ability, Inc.
Book Designer: Felicia Macheske

Photo Credits: © sergemi/Shutterstock.com, cover, 1; © maxsattana/Shutterstock.com, cover, 1; © STILLFX/ Shutterstock.com, cover, 1; Library of Congress, LC-DIG-pga-01711, 5; © Adam Otvos/Shutterstock.com, 6; Library of Congress, LC-DIG-pga-12397, 11; © spetenfia/Shutterstock.com, 12; © Anneka/Shutterstock.com, 17; © Pixeljoy/Shutterstock.com, 18; Library of Congress, LC-DIG-det-4a26642, 21; © Joseph M. Arseneau/ Shutterstock.com, 23; Library of Congress, LC-DIG-pga-08593, 25; © Keith J Finks/Shutterstock.com, 29

Graphic Elements Throughout: © Chipmunk131/Shutterstock.com; © Nowik Sylwia/Shutterstock.com; © Andrey_Popov/Shutterstock.com; © NadzeyaShanchuk/Shutterstock.com; © KathyGold/Shutterstock.com; © Black creator/Shutterstock.com; © Edvard Molnar/Shutterstock.com; © Elenadesign/Shutterstock.com; © estherpoon/Shutterstock.com

45th Parallel Press is an imprint of Cherry Lake Publishing.

Library of Congress Cataloging-in-Publication Data

Names: Loh-Hagan, Virginia, author.
Title: Boycotting the British : Boston Tea Party / by Virginia Loh-Hagan.
Description: [Ann Arbor, MI : Cherry Lake Publishing, 2019] | Series: Behind the curtain | Includes bibliographical references and index. | Audience: Grade 4-6.
Identifiers: LCCN 2018035565| ISBN 9781534143388 (hardcover) | ISBN 9781534139947 (pbk.) | ISBN 9781534141148 (pdf) | ISBN 9781534142343 (hosted ebook)
Subjects: LCSH: Boston Tea Party, Boston, Mass., 1773—Juvenile literature.
Classification: LCC E215.7 .L65 2019 | DDC 973.3/115—dc23
LC record available at https://lccn.loc.gov/2018035565

Cherry Lake Publishing would like to acknowledge the work of The Partnership for 21st Century Skills. Please visit www.p21.org for more information.

Printed in the United States of America
Corporate Graphics

A Note on Dramatic Retellings

Participating in Readers Theater, or dramatic retellings, can greatly improve reading skills, especially fluency. The books in the **BEHIND THE CURTAIN** series give readers opportunities to learn about important historical events in a fun and engaging way. These books serve as a bridge to more complex texts. All the characters are real figures from history; however, their stories have been fictionalized. To learn more about the people and the events, check out the Viewpoints and Perspectives series and the Perspectives Library series, as the **BEHIND THE CURTAIN** books are aligned to these stories.

TABLE of CONTENTS

HISTORICAL BACKGROUND

At first, Great Britain owned the 13 colonies. The British government forced many taxes and laws onto the colonists. Colonists thought these taxes and laws were unfair. They wanted to be their own country. They fought the British. This war was called the American Revolution. It was fought from 1775 to 1783. The American colonists won. They became the United States of America.

The Boston Tea Party took place on December 16, 1773. It was an important event. It led to the war.

The British government needed money. It had fought in wars. It tried to make money by taxing the colonists. It passed the Tea Act. It did this in 1773.

FLASH FACT!
Colonists fought against the Stamp Act.

Vocabulary

colonies (KAH-luh-neez) areas controlled by another country

colonists (KAH-luh-nists) people who live in colonies

revolution (rev-uh-LOO-shuhn) an overthrow of a government

act (AKT) law

FLASH FACT!

The colonists dumped enough tea to fill 18.8 million tea bags.

Vocabulary

protested (PROH-test-id) objected strongly to something

liberty (LIB-ur-tee) freedom

docked (DOKD) anchored a ship near land

The Tea Act forced colonists to buy tea only from the East India Company. This meant that Boston's tea sellers wouldn't make any money. Colonists also had to pay taxes. They were upset. They didn't like laws being passed without their say. They refused to obey the law. They protested. Some colonist leaders formed the Sons of Liberty. This is a group that fought for freedom.

Three ships docked in Boston. They had 90,000 pounds (40,823 kilograms) of tea. Colonists dressed up like Native Americans. They got on board the ships. They chopped open 342 boxes of tea. They threw the tea into the water. This took about 3 hours. This event became known as the Boston Tea Party.

CAST of CHARACTERS

NARRATOR: person who helps tell the story

ANN CLERK: American colonist who is loyal to Great Britain, wife of an East India Company **merchant**

THOMAS HUTCHINSON: royal governor of Massachusetts

THOMAS BRAYSON: British soldier assigned to bring order to Boston

JONATHAN PIERCE: American colonist who is a **patriot**, member of the Sons of Liberty, newspaper printer

SARAH BRADLEE FULTON: American colonist who supports the Boston Tea Party, wife and sister of the Boston Tea Party participants

JOHN CRANE: Boston Tea Party **participant**, soldier, **carpenter**

BACKSTORY
SPOTLIGHT BIOGRAPHY

Penelope Barker was born on June 17, 1728. She was born in Edenton, North Carolina. She was one of the richest women in North Carolina. She was a loyal patriot. She helped support the American Revolution. She organized the Edenton Tea Party. On October 25, 1774, Barker hosted a tea party at a friend's house. Over 50 women were there. The women agreed to not buy British tea. They signed a contract. They protested the Tea Act. They made their own tea. They used leaves and herbs from their gardens. Their gardens were called Liberty Gardens. This was the first recorded women's political protest in the United States. An organized women's movement was not common. It shocked Great Britain. British people made fun of the women. But the colonists were proud of them.

Vocabulary

merchant (MUR-chuhnt) seller or trader

patriot (PAY-tree-uht) an American colonist who wants independence from British rule

participant (pahr-TIS-uh-puhnt) a person who takes part in something

carpenter (KAHR-puhn-tur) a person who makes things out of wood

FLASH FACT!

Samuel Adams was a founding member of the Sons of Liberty.

9

ACT 1

NARRATOR: *It's December 1773. It's a few days before the Boston Tea Party.* **ANN CLERK** *and* **THOMAS HUTCHINSON** *are at the Clerks' tea shop.*

ANN: Things are bad. Someone broke into our shop. This is the third time this month. It's like we live in a **lawless** land. You're the governor. Isn't there anything you can do?

THOMAS H.: These Sons of Liberty are such a pain. They've **threatened** several other merchants. They don't want people to sell British things. They don't want people to buy British things.

ANN: Last week, I heard they poured hot tar on **Loyalist** merchants. Then, they covered them with feathers.

THOMAS H.: How awful! They've also destroyed **property**.

ANN: I don't understand why they're so mad. It's our **duty** to pay taxes.

Vocabulary

lawless (LAW-les) disorder, confusion, wild

threatened (THRET-uhnd) promised to harm

Loyalist (LOI-uhl-ist) person loyal to the king of Great Britain

property (PRAH-pur-tee) land and things owned by people

duty (DOO-tee) job or responsibility

FLASH FACT!
Patriot mobs sometimes tarred and feathered Loyalists.

THOMAS H.: Great Britain fought the Seven Years' War for us. They spent a lot of money. We need to pay them back. That seems fair to me.

ANN: I agree. The British soldiers were protecting us. They were defending the colonies.

THOMAS H.: I wish more people were like you, Ann. We need to be loyal to the king.

ANN: This tea tax worries me, though. People seem to be really upset about it.

THOMAS H.: Hopefully, these patriots will come to their senses. They'll realize that British rule is good for them. Speaking of tea, can I get a cup?

ANN: Sure. Yes. I'll get you some. But we're running low.

THOMAS H.: Don't worry. I checked with the East India Company. We have three big **shipments** coming in.

Vocabulary
shipments (SHIP-muhnts)
supplies that are shipped from one place to another

FLASH FACT!
Colonists found ways to avoid buying British things. For example, they spun their own wool.

NARRATOR: JONATHAN PIERCE *is working in his print shop.* THOMAS BRAYSON *walks in. It's a few hours before the Boston Tea Party.*

THOMAS B.: Stop what you're doing!

JONATHAN: You can't tell me what to do. You're a **Bloody Back**!

THOMAS B.: You're a Son of Liberty. Are you printing things that disobey our king?

JONATHAN: I'm printing newspapers. It's my duty to tell the truth. And the truth is the British are being unfair. We want to be free of British rule.

THOMAS B.: You should be **ashamed** of yourself. My friend said he was attacked. Sons of Liberty threw things at him.

JONATHAN: You don't know the whole story. I was there. The British soldier knocked down a colonist. He did it with his gun. Then more soldiers came. They shot a colonist in the back. I carried him to the doctor. But it was too late. He died.

LOCATION SHOOTING
REAL-WORLD SETTING

The Boston Tea Party took place at Griffin's Wharf. Wharf means pier or dock. Griffin's Wharf is in Boston Harbor. It's no longer there. The land was filled in. Boston Harbor is in Massachusetts Bay. It's in the city of Boston. It has an inner harbor and an outer harbor. It has 180 miles (290 kilometers) of beaches. It has 34 islands. Captain John Smith discovered it in 1614. By 1660, almost all goods were shipped to and from Boston Harbor. This turned Boston into a big city. The first American lighthouse was built in Boston Harbor. It's called Boston Light. It was built in 1716. During the American Revolution, the British captured the lighthouse. The colonists attacked it twice. They burned it. The British blew it up in 1776. The lighthouse was rebuilt in 1783. Today, it's 98 feet (30 meters) tall.

Vocabulary

Bloody Back (BLUHD-ee BAK) a bad name for British soldiers because they wore red uniforms

ashamed (uh-SHAYMD) feeling guilty or embarrassed

FLASH FACT!

The Sons of Liberty met. They talked about ways to fight against British rule.

THOMAS B.: The law will take care of this.

JONATHAN: The law did nothing. The soldiers went to court. They were let go. Nobody from Boston was in the **jury**. That's not fair.

THOMAS B.: Do you think it's better to take the law in your own hands?

JONATHAN: All I'm doing is fighting for liberty. Taxing us without our say is not right.

THOMAS B.: People in Great Britain have to pay taxes. I have no problem paying taxes. So, why do you?

JONATHAN: Paying taxes isn't the real problem. We want a voice in government. We want **representation**. We want freedom to rule ourselves.

THOMAS B.: But …

JONATHAN: Oh no! Look at the time. I have to go. There's somewhere I need to be.

Vocabulary

jury (JOOR-ee) a group of peers who judge others

representation (rep-rih-zen-TAY-shuhn) the state of having an elected person acting on the behalf of others

FLASH FACT!

Part of the Stamp Act said colonists could be tried for crimes without a jury. This made colonists mad.

NARRATOR: JONATHAN PIERCE *and* THOMAS HUTCHINSON *are at the docks. It's a couple of hours before the Boston Tea Party.*

THOMAS H.: I'm the governor. And I'm telling you to leave right now. The Sons of Liberty have no right to be here.

JONATHAN: We're not going anywhere. We take our orders from Samuel Adams.

THOMAS H.: What does he want?

JONATHAN: He wants you to send the ships back to Great Britain.

THOMAS H.: I'm not doing that. The ships stay. The taxes will be paid.

JONATHAN: We're standing guard. We're not paying the taxes. We'll be here day and night. No tea can leave this dock.

THOMAS H.: Merchants are willing to pay the taxes. The taxes aren't even that much money.

JONATHAN: That's not the point. No **taxation** without representation!

Vocabulary
taxation (tak-SAY-shuhn) the process of making others pay taxes

FLASH FACT!
Thomas Hutchinson's house was destroyed in 1765. Patriots stole his belongings.

ACT 2

NARRATOR: *It's an hour before the Boston Tea Party.* **JOHN CRANE** *is at* **SARAH BRADLEE FULTON'S** *house. Sons of Liberty are getting ready.*

SARAH: Did anyone find out about our plans?

JOHN: No. It's top secret. The governor doesn't have a clue.

SARAH: That's good. I'm so proud of you all. My husband and brother are already dressed. They're heading to the ships now.

JOHN: I can't wait to meet up with them. I'm excited and scared at the same time. What we're doing is dangerous.

SARAH: It's an act of **treason**. But our freedom is worth it.

JOHN: Whose idea was it to dress like Mohawk Indians?

SARAH: It was my idea! I thought you all needed a **disguise**. Let's paint your face. Let's get you dressed.

Vocabulary

treason (TREE-zuhn) betrayal, an act against the government

disguise (dis-GIZE) clothes that change how someone looks

FLASH FACT!

The colonists weren't trying to steal the tea. They wanted to destroy it. They didn't want it to be sold.

NARRATOR: JOHN CRANE *meets* **JONATHAN PIERCE** *at the ships. The other Sons of Liberty are there as well. The Boston Tea Party is about to start.*

JOHN: Hi, Jonathan. Here's some coal dust and dark face paint. Sarah sent it. She said to put it on.

JONATHAN: I'll do that right now.

JOHN: Any word on the governor?

JONATHAN: He's not on our side. He won't change his mind. He thinks we should pay the taxes.

JOHN: That's too bad. Boston Harbor will be a **teapot** tonight!

JONATHAN: Shh! Keep your voice down. We don't want the soldiers to hear us.

JOHN: Everyone's here. It's time! We need to split into three groups. One group for each ship.

JONATHAN: It's so dark. It's hard to see.

JOHN: Remember, only destroy the tea. Leave everything else on board.

CAPACITY
227 GALLONS
2 QUARTS
1 PINT
3 GILLS

Vocabulary
teapot (TEE-paht) a pot that makes tea

FLASH FACT!
The Boston Tea Party was not called that until 1825.

NARRATOR: *The Sons of Liberty take their axes. They open up boxes of tea. They dump the tea into the water.* **JOHN CRANE** *goes deep into a ship. He sees more boxes of tea. He gets hit in the head. He wakes up at* **SARAH'S** *house.*

SARAH: Oh, thank goodness! John, you're finally awake. We were so scared.

JOHN: What happened?

SARAH: A box fell on you. The Sons of Liberty hid you. They put you under a pile of wood pieces. Jonathan returned to get you. He carried you here. We thought you were dead.

Vocabulary
evidence (EV-ih-duhns) proof

FLASH FACT!
Some colonists watched the Boston Tea Party from the shore.

JOHN: Did we do it? Did we dump the tea?

SARAH: Yes, it's done. All 342 boxes of tea! All gone! But now it's time to get you cleaned up. We have to get rid of the **evidence**.

JOHN: Before I got hit, I heard Samuel Adams say something. He said, "With ladies on our side, we can make the **Tories tremble**."

SARAH: That's nice to hear. Women and men need to work together for freedom.

NARRATOR: *The Boston Tea Party just ended.* **THOMAS BRAYSON** *runs to* **THOMAS HUTCHINSON'S** *house.*

THOMAS B.: All the tea is destroyed. Not one penny in taxes have been paid.

THOMAS H.: How much damage is there?

THOMAS B.: The Sons of Liberty didn't harm the ships. They didn't take any tea for themselves. They left all the other things.

THOMAS H.: Why didn't our soldiers stop them?

THOMAS B.: We never got orders.

THOMAS H.: The king will be mad. He'll make their lives **intolerable**.

BLOOPERS
HISTORICAL MISTAKES

Patriots believed in "liberty and property." George Washington was the first U.S. president. He was also the leader of the army. He thought the Boston Tea Party was a bad move. He disagreed with "their conduct in destroying the tea." Conduct means behavior. Washington thought the Boston Tea Party people were "mad," or crazy. He thought they destroyed private property. He thought they should pay back the East India Company. Benjamin Franklin was also one of the Founding Fathers. He felt the same way. The Boston Tea Party people threw over $1 million of tea into the water. Not everyone agreed with the Boston Tea Party. But the colonists agreed that Great Britain's reaction was bad. Great Britain punished the colonists. It passed laws. It closed Boston's port. It took away the colonists' rights. It thought this would stop the colonists. But this angered the colonists. They went to war.

Vocabulary

Tories (TOR-eez) Americans who supported British rule

tremble (TREM-buhl) to shake out of fear

intolerable (in-TAH-lur-uh-buhl) too hard to handle because of extreme hardship

FLASH FACT!
British soldiers weren't present during the Boston Tea Party.

THOMAS B.: Those patriots deserve it. They can't get away with this.

THOMAS H.: There will be war. I need to hide. I'll go to Castle William.

THOMAS B.: What's Castle William?

THOMAS H.: It's a British fort. It's on an island in Boston Harbor. You should come with me. Things aren't going to be safe for Loyalists in Boston.

NARRATOR: ANN CLERK and **THOMAS HUTCHINSON** *see each other at Castle William. It's a few days after the Boston Tea Party.*

THOMAS H.: What brings you here, Ann?

ANN: Things got really bad. The Sons of Liberty surrounded my house. They howled. They said they'd hurt us. Then, they came to the tea shop. They called us **traitors**. They threw stones. They broke our windows.

THOMAS H.: They'll pay for what they've done.

ANN: These men are fighting for freedom. They'll find a way to win.

Vocabulary

traitors (TRAY-turz)
people who betray

FLASH FACT!
Castle William housed Loyalists. While the castle was later destroyed, the island it was on is preserved as a state park today.

EVENT TIMELINE

April 5, 1764: The British government passes the Sugar Act. Colonists have to pay taxes on sugar items.

September 1, 1764: The British government passes the Currency Act. Currency means money. Colonists can't make their own money.

March 22, 1765: The British government passes the Stamp Act. This law put a tax on all paper items. This is the first direct tax on the colonists. It ends in 1766.

March 24, 1765: The British government passes the Quartering Act. Quartering means providing food and shelter. Colonists have to let British soldiers stay in their homes.

August 1765: The Sons of Liberty is formed. This is a secret group. They fight against unfair British laws. In Boston, Samuel Adams leads the Sons of Liberty.

October 1765: The Stamp Act Congress takes place. They protest British taxes. They fight against "taxation without representation." They refuse to buy British things.

1767–1768: The British government passes the Townshend Acts. Colonists have to pay taxes on glass, lead, paint, paper, and tea. Colonists protest. The Townshend Acts are cut back in 1770.

May 10, 1773: The British government passes the Tea Act.

August 4, 1773: Seven Loyalist merchants in Boston are chosen to sell tea. The tea is provided by the East India Company.

November 28, 1773: The *Dartmouth* is a ship. It docks in Boston Harbor. It carries the first shipment of tea. The *Beaver* and the *Eleanor* also dock a couple of weeks later. The Sons of Liberty appoint 25 men to guard the ships. They make sure none of the tea is taken off the ships.

December 16, 1773: The Boston Tea Party takes place.

March 1774: The British government passes the Coercive Acts. Coercive means being forceful. These laws punish colonists for not obeying British rule. The colonists call these laws the Intolerable Acts.

CONSIDER THIS!

TAKE A POSITION! Learn more about the Boston Tea Party. Should the American colonists have destroyed the tea? Do you agree with the British or the American colonists? Argue your point with reasons and evidence.

SAY WHAT? Learn more about the Boston Tea Party. Explain the causes of the Boston Tea Party. Explain the effects of the Boston Tea Party.

THINK ABOUT IT! Think about some of the laws that affect you. Which laws do you think are unfair? What is the purpose of the laws? Why do you think they're unfair? How can you protest the laws? Read about peaceful protests.

LEARN MORE

Brennan, Linda Crotta. *The Boston Tea Party*. Ann Arbor, MI: Cherry Lake Publishing, 2014.

Freedman, Russell. *The Boston Tea Party*. New York: Holiday House, 2012.

Krull, Kathleen. *A Kid's Guide to the American Revolution*. New York: HarperCollins, 2018.

Krull, Kathleen. *What Was the Boston Tea Party?* New York: Grosset & Dunlap, 2013.

Russo, Kristin J. *Viewpoints on the Boston Tea Party*. Ann Arbor, MI: Cherry Lake Publishing, 2019.

INDEX

ABOUT THE AUTHOR

Dr. Virginia Loh-Hagan is an author, university professor, and former classroom teacher. She loves drinking unsweetened iced tea. She is addicted to it. She lives in San Diego with her very tall husband and very naughty dogs. To learn more about her, visit www.virginialoh.com.